Brian Mulroney visions

"His Legacy of Leadership and Controversy"

RUDOLF VIRCHOW

Table of contents

Introduction:

Brian Mulroney, the 18th Prime Minister of Canada, left an indelible mark on the nation's political landscape during his tenure from 1984 to 1993. A figure both revered and controversial, Mulroney's leadership spanned significant economic reforms, international relations initiatives, and enduring debates. Born in humble beginnings in Quebec, his journey from a blue-collar town to the highest office in the land reflects the quintessential Canadian narrative of resilience and ambition. This introduction sets the stage for exploring Mulroney's multifaceted biography, his contributions to Canadian society, and the complexities of his legacy.

Throughout his career, Mulroney navigated the complexities of domestic politics and international diplomacy with equal vigor. His landmark achievements include the negotiation of the North American Free Trade Agreement (NAFTA), which reshaped the economic landscape of North America. Additionally, Mulroney's advocacy for environmental issues, such as combating acid rain, showcased his commitment to global cooperation on pressing environmental challenges. However, Mulroney's tenure was not without controversy. The introduction of the Goods and Services Tax (GST) and the privatization of Crown corporations sparked public outcry and political opposition. Moreover, revelations of financial dealings with controversial figures tarnished his reputation and raised questions about ethics in government. Despite the controversies, Mulroney's legacy endures as a pivotal figure in Canadian history. His leadership during a period of significant economic and geopolitical change left an indelible imprint on the nation. This exploration of Mulroney's life and legacy offers insight into the complexities of political leadership and the enduring impact of one man's vision for his country.

Chapter One

Early Life and Career

Brian Mulroney's journey of leadership begins in the picturesque town of Baie-Comeau, nestled in the heart of northeastern Quebec. Born on March 20, 1939, and died on 29 February 2024. Mulroney was raised in a close-knit community surrounded by the natural beauty of the Canadian wilderness. Growing up in a blue-collar family, Mulroney learned the virtues of hard work, perseverance, and resilience from his parents. His father, Benedict, worked as an electrician in the local paper mill, while his mother, Irene, devoted herself to caring for Brian and his four siblings.

Brian Mulroney's wife is Mila Mulroney, and they have four children: Caroline Mulroney – She is a politician in Ontario, Canada Mulroney – He is a well-known television presenter in Canada. Mark Mulroney Nicolas Mulroney.

Despite the challenges of their modest circumstances, Mulroney's parents placed a high value on education and encouraged their children to pursue their dreams. From an early age, Mulroney exhibited a keen intellect and a thirst for knowledge, eagerly devouring books and immersing himself in the world of ideas. The rugged landscape of Baie-Comeau provided a backdrop for Mulroney's formative years, instilling in him a deep appreciation for the natural world and a sense of connection to his surroundings. The rugged coastline, dense forests, and pristine rivers served as both playground and classroom, shaping Mulroney's outlook on life and his understanding of the importance of preserving the environment for future generations. As Mulroney matured, he began to recognize the opportunities that lay beyond the confines of his small hometown. Inspired by his parents' unwavering support and his own aspirations for a brighter future, Mulroney set his sights on higher education and the pursuit of his dreams.

The early years In Baie-Comeau laid the foundation for Mulroney's remarkable journey, instilling in him the values of hard work, determination, and community that would guide him throughout his life. From the rugged shores of northeastern Quebec to the corridors of power in Ottawa, Brian Mulroney's origins in Baie-Comeau remain a testament to the power of resilience and the pursuit of excellence.

As Mulroney continued to mature in Baie-Comeau, he witnessed firsthand the struggles and triumphs of his community. The resilience of the townsfolk in the face of economic challenges left a lasting impression on him, shaping his understanding of the importance of community solidarity and collective action. Despite the limited resources available in his hometown, Mulroney's parents emphasized the value of education as a pathway to success. They encouraged their children to excel academically and to pursue their ambitions with determination and perseverance. Mulroney's own academic pursuits were marked by dedication and commitment. He excelled in his studies, demonstrating a keen intellect and a natural aptitude for learning. His teachers recognized his potential early on, nurturing his talents and instilling in him a sense of confidence and self-assurance. Beyond the classroom, Mulroney's upbringing in Baie-Comeau instilled in him a strong work ethic and a sense of responsibility to his community. He took on part-time jobs during his teenage years, working alongside his father at the paper mill and taking on odd jobs to help support his family. These formative experiences imbued Mulroney with a deep appreciation for the value of hard work and the importance of giving back to others. They laid the groundwork for his future endeavors in law, politics, and public service, shaping his character and guiding his actions as he embarked on his journey of leadership. As Mulroney reflects on his upbringing in Baie-Comeau, he recognizes the profound influence that his hometown had on shaping his values, aspirations, and sense of purpose. It was here, amid the rugged beauty of northeastern Quebec, that the seeds of leadership were sown, setting him on a path that would ultimately lead him to the highest office in the land.

In conclusion, Brian Mulroney's early life in Baie-Comeau laid the groundwork for his journey of leadership. Raised in a close-knit community marked by hard work, resilience, and a strong sense of community, Mulroney developed the values and character traits that would shape his future endeavors. His upbringing instilled in him a deep appreciation for education, a commitment to social justice, and a reverence for the environment. Moreover, the support and guidance of his parents, coupled with the opportunities and challenges of growing up in a small paper mill town, cultivated Mulroney's ambition and drive to succeed. His experiences in Baie-Comeau fueled his determination to make a difference in the world and to contribute to the betterment of his community and country. As Mulroney reflects on his origins in Baie-Comeau, he acknowledges the profound impact that his hometown had on shaping his values, aspirations, and sense of purpose. It was here, amid the rugged beauty of northeastern Quebec, that the seeds of leadership were sown, setting him on a path that would ultimately lead him to become one of Canada's most influential political figures.In the subsequent chapters of this ebook, we will explore how Mulroney's early life experiences informed his career in law, his entry into politics, and his rise to prominence as Prime Minister of Canada. We will examine the key moments, decisions, and challenges that shaped his leadership style and legacy, offering insights into the man behind the politician and the enduring impact of his leadership on the nation

Chapter Two

The Path to Law and Politics

After completing his education at Laval University in Quebec City, Brian Mulroney embarked on a journey that would lead him to the intersection of law and politics. Armed with a degree in law, Mulroney's keen intellect and ambition propelled him into a successful legal career. Mulroney's experiences as a lawyer provided him with invaluable insights into the workings of the legal system and the complexities of the intersection between law and politics. His legal expertise and sharp analytical skills positioned him as a formidable figure in the legal community, earning him respect and recognition among his peers.In 1974, Mulroney's trajectory took a pivotal turn when he was tapped to participate in a commission investigating organized crime's infiltration of labor unions involved in the James Bay hydroelectric project. This marked his entry into the world of public service and advocacy, as he dedicated himself to uncovering corruption and fighting for justice on behalf of the Canadian people. Mulroney's involvement in the commission showcased his commitment to upholding the rule of law and his willingness to tackle complex and contentious issues head-on. His contributions to the investigation earned him praise for his integrity, diligence, and dedication to serving the public interest. As Mulroney continued to navigate the realms of law and public service, his experiences laid the groundwork for his eventual entry into politics. His passion for justice, coupled with his legal expertise and leadership qualities, positioned him as a natural candidate for political office.In the subsequent chapters of this ebook, we will explore how Brian Mulroney's journey through the worlds of law and public service paved the way for his ascent to the highest office in the land as Prime Minister of Canada. We will delve into the key moments, decisions, and challenges that shaped his political career and his enduring legacy as a transformative figure in Canadian history.

As Mulroney delved deeper into the realm of public service and advocacy through his involvement in the commission investigating organized crime, he became increasingly aware of the power dynamics at play within Canadian society. His experiences shed light on the intricacies of political and legal systems, fueling his desire to effect change from within the corridors of power. Motivated by a sense of duty to serve his country and guided by his strong moral compass, Mulroney began to contemplate a transition into the realm of politics. Recognizing the potential to enact meaningful reform and address pressing issues facing Canadians, he set his sights on a new frontier: the political arena. Mulroney's decision to enter politics was driven by a deep-seated belief in the importance of public service and a desire to make a positive impact on the lives of his fellow citizens. His experiences as a lawyer and advocate equipped him with the skills, knowledge, and determination needed to navigate the complexities of the political landscape.In 1983, Mulroney took the plunge and declared his candidacy for a parliamentary seat representing Nova Scotia. His decision to run for office marked a significant turning point in his career, as he transitioned from legal advocate to political candidate.Mulroney's campaign resonated with voters, who were drawn to his message of integrity, leadership, and vision for a better Canada. His ability to connect with Canadians from all walks of life and articulate a compelling vision for the future propelled him to victory in the federal election, securing him a seat in Parliament. As Mulroney settled into his new role as a Member of Parliament, he remained committed to his core principles of honesty, integrity, and dedication to public service. His journey from the halls of academia to the chambers of Parliament was a testament to his unwavering commitment to serving the interests of Canadians and building a better future for generations to come. In the chapters that follow, we will continue to explore Brian Mulroney's ascent in the world of politics, tracing his path to leadership and examining the key moments, decisions, and challenges that shaped his remarkable career. From his early days as a legal advocate to his tenure as Prime Minister of Canada, Mulroney's journey is a testament to the power of determination, resilience, and unwavering dedication to the public good.

As Mulroney continued his political journey, he quickly established himself as a rising star within the Progressive Conservative Party. His sharp intellect, charismatic demeanor, and unwavering commitment to Canadian values resonated with both party members and voters alike.With each passing year, Mulroney's influence within the party grew stronger, culminating in his election as the leader of the Progressive Conservatives in 1983. This pivotal moment marked the beginning of a new chapter in Mulroney's political career, as he assumed the mantle of leadership and embarked on a mission to revitalize the party and lead it to victory in the federal election. Under Mulroney's leadership, the Progressive Conservatives underwent a period of renewal and reinvigoration, with a focus on modernization, unity, and inclusivity. His strategic vision and ability to inspire loyalty and confidence among party members helped to galvanize support and propel the party to new heights of success. In the 1984 federal election, Mulroney led the Progressive Conservatives to a landslide victory, defeating the incumbent Liberal government and securing a majority mandate. His victory was a testament to his leadership skills, political acumen, and ability to connect with voters on a personal level.As Prime Minister of Canada, Mulroney wasted no time in setting his agenda for the nation. His vision for Canada was one of economic prosperity, social justice, and national unity. He embarked on a series of ambitious reforms aimed at stimulating economic growth, creating jobs, and enhancing Canada's global competitiveness. From the negotiation of the landmark Canada-U.S. Free Trade Agreement to the implementation of sweeping tax reforms, Mulroney's tenure as Prime Minister was characterized by bold and decisive action. His leadership style was marked by pragmatism, determination, and a relentless pursuit of excellence. In the chapters that follow, we will delve deeper into Mulroney's achievements as Prime Minister, examining the key policies, initiatives, and challenges that defined his time in office. From his efforts to strengthen Canada's economy to his commitment to social justice and environmental stewardship, Mulroney's legacy as a transformative leader continues to resonate with Canadians to this day.

Throughout his as Prime Minister, Brian Mulroney's leadership was characterized by a relentless commitment to advancing the interests of Canadians on both the domestic and international fronts. One of his most notable achievements was the negotiation and implementation of the North American Free Trade Agreement (NAFTA), which fundamentally reshaped the economic landscape of North America and positioned Canada for greater prosperity on the global stage. Mulroney's vision for NAFTA stemmed from his belief in the power of free trade to stimulate economic growth, create jobs, and enhance the competitiveness of

Canadian industries. Despite facing opposition and skepticism from various quarters, Mulroney remained steadfast in his determination to secure a trade agreement with Canada's largest trading partner, the United States. After months of intense negotiations, Mulroney succeeded in finalizing the NAFTA agreement with the United States and Mexico in 1992. The historic trade deal eliminated tariffs and trade barriers between the three countries, opening up new opportunities for businesses and consumers and fostering deeper economic integration across North America. The implementation of NAFTA had a profound impact on Canada's economy, leading to increased trade, investment, and job creation in key sectors such as manufacturing, agriculture, and services. Mulroney's foresight and leadership in championing free trade laid the groundwork for Canada's emergence as a global economic powerhouse in the years to come. In addition to his achievements in economic policy, Mulroney's tenure as Prime Minister was also marked by significant strides in environmental stewardship and social justice. He played a key role in international efforts to combat acid rain, advocating for greater cooperation and environmental protection measures among nations. Furthermore, Mulroney demonstrated a commitment to social justice and equality through his support for initiatives aimed at addressing poverty, homelessness, and discrimination. His government's implementation of the Canadian Charter of Rights and Freedoms reinforced Canada's commitment to upholding fundamental human rights and freedoms for all citizens.

Chapter Three

Rise to Power

Brian Mulroney's rise to power within the Progressive Conservative Party marked a pivotal moment in Canadian politics. As he assumed the leadership of the party, Mulroney embarked on a mission to revitalize its fortunes and lead it to victory in the federal election. Mulroney's leadership style was characterized by charisma, strategic vision, and an unwavering commitment to Canadian values. He understood the importance of party unity and worked tirelessly to bridge divides within the Progressive Conservative Party, rallying members around a shared vision for the future.Under Mulroney's leadership, the Progressive Conservatives underwent a period of renewal and reinvigoration. He implemented organizational reforms, modernized the party's platform, and cultivated a sense of optimism and momentum among party members and supporters. In the 1984 federal election, Mulroney led the Progressive Conservatives to a landslide victory, defeating the incumbent Liberal government and securing a majority mandate. His victory was a testament to his leadership skills, political acumen, and ability to connect with voters on a personal level.As Prime Minister of Canada, Mulroney wasted no time in setting his agenda for the nation. His vision for Canada was one of economic prosperity, social justice, and national unity. He embarked on a series of ambitious reforms aimed at stimulating economic growth, creating jobs, and enhancing Canada's global competitiveness.From the negotiation of the landmark Canada-U.S. Free Trade Agreement to the implementation of sweeping tax reforms, Mulroney's tenure as Prime Minister was characterized by bold and decisive action. His leadership style was marked by pragmatism, determination, and a relentless pursuit of excellence. In addition to his achievements in economic policy, Mulroney's tenure as Prime Minister was also marked by significant strides in environmental stewardship and social justice. He played a key role in international efforts to combat acid rain, advocating for greater cooperation and environmental protection measures among nations. Furthermore, Mulroney demonstrated a commitment to social justice and equality through his support for initiatives aimed at addressing poverty, homelessness, and discrimination. His government's implementation of the Canadian Charter of Rights and Freedoms reinforced Canada's commitment to upholding fundamental human rights and freedoms for all citizens. In summary, Brian Mulroney's legacy as Prime Minister is defined by his bold leadership, visionary policymaking, and unwavering dedication to advancing the interests of Canadians at home and abroad. From his pivotal role in negotiating NAFTA to his efforts to promote environmental sustainability and social justice, Mulroney's impact on Canada's political, economic, and social landscape continues to be felt to this day.

As Prime Minister, Brian Mulroney faced a myriad of challenges and opportunities on both the domestic and international fronts. One of his foremost priorities was to address Canada's economic landscape and promote growth and prosperity for all Canadians. Mulroney's economic agenda was multifaceted, encompassing measures aimed at reducing deficits, stimulating investment, and fostering innovation. His government implemented significant tax reforms, including the introduction of the Goods and Services Tax (GST), which aimed to modernize Canada's tax system and generate revenue for government programs. In addition to tax reform, Mulroney pursued deregulation and privatization initiatives to spur economic growth and enhance competitiveness. He oversaw the privatization of several Crown corporations, including Air Canada, in an effort to increase efficiency and reduce government intervention in the economy. Mulroney also prioritized free trade agreements as a means to expand Canada's economic opportunities on the global stage. In addition to NAFTA, he negotiated the Canada-U.S. Free Trade Agreement, which laid the groundwork for deeper economic integration between the two countries and paved the way for NAFTA's eventual implementation. While Mulroney's economic policies were met with both praise and criticism, there is no denying their lasting impact on Canada's economic landscape. The reforms implemented during his tenure set the stage for sustained economic growth and prosperity in the years that followed, solidifying Canada's position as a competitive player in the global economy. In addition to his economic agenda, Mulroney's government also pursued initiatives aimed at promoting social justice and equality. He championed the rights of Indigenous peoples, implementing measures to address longstanding issues such as land claims and self-governance. Mulroney's commitment to social justice extended to his support for multiculturalism and diversity, as well as his efforts to combat discrimination and promote inclusivity. His government passed legislation to protect the rights of minority groups and promote equality of opportunity for all Canadians. Furthermore, Mulroney's tenure as Prime Minister was characterized by a proactive approach to foreign relations, marked by a commitment to diplomacy, peacekeeping, and international cooperation. He played a key role in efforts to address global challenges such as climate change, nuclear disarmament, and human rights violations.

Chapter Four

Prime Ministerial Tenure and Policy Initiatives

Upon assuming office as Prime Minister in 1984, Brian Mulroney faced a myriad of challenges and opportunities, both domestically and internationally. His tenure was marked by bold policy initiatives and significant geopolitical developments that left an indelible mark on Canada's history. One of Mulroney's most notable achievements was the negotiation and implementation of the North American Free Trade Agreement (NAFTA). Recognizing the potential for economic integration and trade liberalization, Mulroney spearheaded negotiations between Canada, the United States, and Mexico, culminating in the historic agreement in 1994. NAFTA not only facilitated increased trade and investment but also positioned Canada as a key player in the global economy. In addition to NAFTA, Mulroney pursued an ambitious agenda of domestic reforms aimed at modernizing Canada's economy and advancing social progress. His government introduced sweeping changes to taxation, privatization, and social welfare programs, with the goal of promoting fiscal responsibility and economic growth. Mulroney's economic policies, however, were not without controversy. The introduction of the Goods and Services Tax (GST) in 1991 sparked public outcry and political opposition. Critics argued that the tax disproportionately burdened low-income Canadians and exacerbated social inequalities. Despite the backlash, Mulroney defended the GST as a necessary measure to address budget deficits and ensure long-term economic stability. In addition to economic reforms, Mulroney's government tackled pressing social issues, including the environment and Indigenous rights. His administration took steps to address the proliferation of acid rain and pollution, implementing measures to protect Canada's natural habitats and promote sustainable development. Internationally, Mulroney played a significant role in shaping Canada's foreign policy agenda. He strengthened Canada's ties with key allies, particularly the United States, while also advocating for global cooperation on issues such as nuclear disarmament and human rights. Overall, Brian Mulroney's tenure as Prime Minister was characterized by bold leadership and decisive action. His policy initiatives, though controversial at times, reflected his commitment to modernizing Canada's economy and promoting its interests on the world stage. Despite facing challenges and criticism, Mulroney's legacy as a transformative leader endures, leaving an indelible mark on the fabric of Canadian society.

Throughout his tenure as Prime Minister, Brian Mulroney demonstrated a keen understanding of the interconnectedness of domestic and international affairs, leveraging Canada's position on the global stage to advance its interests while navigating complex geopolitical landscapes. One of the defining aspects of Mulroney's leadership was his approach to Indigenous rights and reconciliation. Recognizing the historical injustices faced by Indigenous peoples, Mulroney's government sought to address these issues through dialogue and negotiation. In 1987, Mulroney delivered a landmark speech in the House of Commons, acknowledging the need for a new relationship between the Canadian government and Indigenous communities. This marked the beginning of a series of initiatives aimed at advancing Indigenous rights and fostering reconciliation, including the establishment of the Royal Commission on Aboriginal Peoples in 1991.Mulroney's commitment to social progress extended beyond Indigenous rights to include efforts to combat discrimination and promote equality for all Canadians. His government passed legislation to protect the rights of women, minorities, and LGBTQ+ individuals, laying the groundwork for a more inclusive and equitable society. On the international front, Mulroney played a pivotal role in shaping Canada's response to global challenges. He championed multilateralism and diplomacy, advocating for Canada's participation in international peacekeeping missions and efforts to address humanitarian crises around the world. Mulroney's leadership during the end of the Cold War era was particularly noteworthy, as he worked to strengthen ties with both Western allies and former adversaries, fostering a climate of cooperation and dialogue. Despite his many accomplishments, Mulroney's tenure as Prime Minister was not without its challenges. Economic downturns, regional tensions, and political controversies tested his leadership at various points during his time in office. However, Mulroney's ability to navigate these challenges with pragmatism and resilience ensured that Canada remained on course towards greater prosperity and stability.

Despite facing challenges and controversies during his time in office, Brian Mulroney's legacy as Prime Minister of Canada is one of significant achievement and lasting impact. His tenure saw Canada assert itself on the global stage, playing a key role in international affairs while also pursuing ambitious domestic reforms aimed at modernizing the economy and promoting social progress.Mulroney's leadership style was characterized by a combination of pragmatism, vision, and a willingness to tackle difficult issues head-on. He understood the importance of consensus-building and compromise, forging alliances both within Canada and abroad to advance the nation's interests.One of Mulroney's enduring legacies is his role in shaping Canada's relationship with the United States. He worked closely with U.S. President Ronald Reagan and later with President George H.W. Bush to strengthen bilateral ties and promote North American cooperation. The negotiation and implementation of NAFTA stand as a testament to Mulroney's commitment to free trade and economic integration, laying the foundation for decades of prosperity and growth in the region.At home, Mulroney's government implemented bold economic reforms that laid the groundwork for Canada's emergence as a global economic powerhouse. While controversial at the time, measures such as the GST and privatization of state-owned enterprises were aimed at streamlining government operations, reducing deficits, and stimulating investment.Mulroney's commitment to social progress was also evident in his efforts to address issues such as Indigenous rights, gender equality, and environmental protection. His government's support for the United Nations Convention on the Rights of the Child and the Montreal Protocol on Substances that Deplete the

Ozone Layer demonstrated Canada's commitment to global cooperation on pressing environmental and humanitarian issues.In the years since leaving office, Brian Mulroney has continued to be a prominent voice in Canadian public life, advocating for causes such as environmental conservation and international peacekeeping. Despite the controversies and challenges he faced during his time in office, Mulroney's contributions to Canadian politics and his impact on the nation's history remain significant and enduring.

During Brian Mulroney's tenure as Prime Minister, Canada experienced a period of significant economic growth and international prominence. Mulroney's leadership was characterized by a strong commitment to advancing the nation's interests and leveraging its position on the global stage. Here are some advantages and examples of his commitment to Canada:Economic Advancement: Mulroney's government implemented bold economic reforms aimed at modernizing Canada's economy and promoting growth. Initiatives such as the negotiation of NAFTA and the privatization of state-owned enterprises helped stimulate investment, create jobs, and expand Canada's export markets.Global Leadership: Mulroney played a key role in shaping Canada's role in international affairs, advocating for multilateralism, diplomacy, and cooperation. He worked closely with allies such as the United States to address pressing global issues, including nuclear disarmament, environmental protection, and humanitarian crises.Domestic Policy Initiatives: Mulroney's government pursued a wide range of domestic policy initiatives aimed at promoting social progress and equality. Measures such as the Royal Commission on Aboriginal Peoples and legislation to protect the rights of women and minorities demonstrated his commitment to addressing historical injustices and promoting inclusivity.Environmental Stewardship: Mulroney prioritized environmental protection and conservation, recognizing the importance of safeguarding Canada's natural resources for future generations. His government took steps to address issues such as acid rain and pollution, signing international agreements such as the

Montreal Protocol on Substances that Deplete the Ozone Layer. Commitment to Reconciliation: Mulroney's acknowledgment of the need for a new relationship between the Canadian government and Indigenous communities marked a significant step towards reconciliation. His government's efforts to address Indigenous rights and advance Indigenous-led initiatives demonstrated a commitment to healing past injustices and fostering a more inclusive society.

Chapter Five

Challenges and Controversies

Despite his many accomplishments, Brian Mulroney's tenure as Prime Minister was not without its share of challenges and controversies. His ambitious policy agenda and decisive leadership style often sparked public outcry and political opposition, leading to contentious debates and scrutiny.Economic Policies: One of the most significant controversies during Mulroney's tenure was the introduction of the Goods and Services Tax (GST) in 1991. The implementation of this consumption tax faced widespread criticism from the public, who viewed it as regressive and burdensome, particularly on lower-income Canadians. The GST sparked protests and political opposition, contributing to a decline in Mulroney's popularity.Privatization and Economic Restructuring: Mulroney's government pursued a policy of privatization, selling off state-owned enterprises such as Air Canada and Petro-Canada. While proponents argued that privatization would improve efficiency and stimulate competition, critics raised concerns about job losses and the erosion of public services. The privatization agenda fueled tensions between labor unions and the government, leading to strikes and protests. Environmental Issues: Mulroney faced criticism for his government's handling of environmental issues, particularly the proliferation of acid rain and pollution in Canada's natural habitats. Environmentalists accused the government of prioritizing economic interests over environmental protection, leading to tensions and protests. The lack of significant progress on environmental issues during Mulroney's tenure contributed to public disillusionment with his government's policies. International Relations: Mulroney's close relationship with the United States, particularly during the Reagan and Bush administrations, also faced scrutiny and criticism. Critics accused Mulroney of aligning too closely with U.S. interests and sacrificing Canada's sovereignty in the process. His government's support for U.S. policies, such as the Strategic Defense Initiative (SDI), drew criticism from peace activists and anti-nuclear groups. Ethical Concerns: Mulroney's government was plagued by allegations of ethical impropriety and scandals. The Airbus Affair, in which Mulroney was accused of accepting kickbacks in exchange for promoting the sale of Airbus aircraft to Air Canada, tarnished his reputation and led to public inquiries. While Mulroney denied any wrongdoing, the scandal damaged public trust in his government and raised questions about integrity and ethics in Canadian politics.

Scandals and Legal Disputes: In addition to the Airbus Affair, Mulroney's government faced other scandals and legal disputes that tarnished its reputation. Allegations of financial impropriety, including accusations of accepting cash payments from lobbyists and arms dealers, raised questions about Mulroney's integrity and ethics. These scandals led to public inquiries and legal battles, further eroding public trust in the government and its leadership. Media Scrutiny and Public Perception: Mulroney's tenure was marked by intense media scrutiny and negative public perception, fueled in part by the controversies and scandals surrounding his government. Criticism from the media, opposition parties, and civil society organizations contributed to a sense of disillusionment among the Canadian public, who increasingly viewed the government as out of touch and unresponsive to their concerns.Legacy of Division: The controversies and challenges faced by Mulroney's government left a legacy of division and polarization within Canadian society. The Meech Lake and Charlottetown Accords, in particular, highlighted deep-seated divisions along regional and linguistic lines, exacerbating tensions between Quebec and the rest of Canada. The failure to achieve constitutional reform further underscored the challenges of national unity and reconciliation.Impact on Progressive Conservative Party: Mulroney's leadership had a profound impact on the Progressive Conservative Party, both during his tenure and in the years following his departure from office. The party experienced internal divisions and ideological shifts as a result of Mulroney's policies and leadership style. His legacy continues to influence the party's identity and direction, as subsequent leaders grapple with the legacy of his government's policies and controversies.Lessons Learned: Despite the controversies and challenges faced during his tenure, Brian Mulroney's government provides valuable lessons for future leaders and policymakers. His experiences underscore the importance of ethical governance, transparency, and accountability in public office. The Mulroney era serves as a cautionary tale about the pitfalls of political hubris and the consequences of losing public trust.In reflecting on the complexities of Mulroney's legacy, it becomes clear that his tenure as Prime Minister was characterized by both achievements and shortcomings. While his government made significant contributions to Canadian politics and policy-making, it also faced numerous challenges and controversies that continue to shape perceptions of his leadership and legacy. Ultimately, Brian Mulroney's legacy serves as a reminder of the complexities of governance and the enduring importance of integrity, accountability, and public trust in democratic societies.

Chapter Six

Legacy and Post-Political Career

After stepping down as Prime Minister in 1993, Brian Mulroney embarked on a new chapter of his life, leaving behind a legacy that continues to shape Canadian politics and society. Despite the controversies and challenges he faced during his tenure, Mulroney remained active in public life, advocating for causes he believed in and leaving his mark on Canadian history in various ways.Advocacy for Causes: Following his departure from politics, Mulroney continued to be a prominent voice in Canadian public discourse, advocating for causes such as environmental conservation, social justice, and international peacekeeping. He used his platform to raise awareness about pressing issues facing Canada and the world, leveraging his experience and influence to effect positive change.Environmental Conservation: Mulroney's commitment to environmental protection and conservation remained steadfast in his post-political career. He became involved in various initiatives aimed at preserving Canada's natural heritage, advocating for policies to address climate change, protect endangered species, and promote sustainable development. His advocacy helped raise awareness about the importance of environmental stewardship and the need for collective action to safeguard the planet for future generations.Social Justice: Mulroney continued to champion social justice causes, advocating for equality, diversity, and inclusivity in Canadian society. He spoke out against discrimination and injustice, using his voice to support marginalized communities and promote policies to advance human rights and social progress. His efforts helped contribute to a more inclusive and equitable Canada, fostering a culture of tolerance and acceptance.International Peacekeeping: Mulroney remained committed to Canada's tradition of international peacekeeping and diplomacy, advocating for greater Canadian involvement in global peacekeeping efforts. He supported initiatives to resolve conflicts and promote stability in regions affected by violence and conflict, emphasizing the importance of diplomacy and dialogue in resolving international disputes. Legacy and Impact: Despite the controversies and criticisms that marked his tenure as Prime Minister, Brian Mulroney's contributions to Canadian politics and society are undeniable. His leadership during a period of profound change and transformation helped shape the future of Canada and solidified his place in the annals of Canadian history. Mulroney's legacy serves as a reminder of the complexities of leadership and the enduring importance of integrity, vision, and dedication to public service.

Advocacy for Causes: Following his departure from politics, Mulroney continued to be a prominent voice in Canadian public discourse, advocating for causes such as environmental conservation, social justice, and international peacekeeping. He used his platform to raise awareness about pressing issues facing Canada and the world, leveraging his experience and influence to effect positive change.Mulroney's advocacy for environmental conservation was particularly notable. He recognized the importance of protecting Canada's natural heritage and spoke out against threats to the environment, such as climate change and habitat destruction. Mulroney became involved in various initiatives aimed at preserving Canada's biodiversity, advocating for policies to address environmental degradation and promote sustainable development. His efforts helped raise awareness about the importance of environmental stewardship and the need for collective action to safeguard the planet for future generations.In addition to environmental issues, Mulroney continued to champion social justice causes, advocating for equality, diversity, and inclusivity in Canadian society. He spoke out against discrimination and injustice, using his voice to support marginalized communities and promote policies to advance human rights and social progress. Mulroney's advocacy helped contribute to a more inclusive and equitable Canada, fostering a culture of tolerance and acceptance.Mulroney also remained committed to Canada's tradition of international peacekeeping and diplomacy. He advocated for greater Canadian involvement in global peacekeeping efforts, supporting initiatives to resolve conflicts and promote stability in regions affected by violence and conflict. Mulroney emphasized the importance of diplomacy and dialogue in resolving international disputes, and his efforts helped raise Canada's profile as a key player in global affairs.Legacy and Impact: Despite the controversies and criticisms that marked his tenure as Prime Minister, Brian Mulroney's contributions to Canadian politics and society are undeniable. His leadership during a period of profound change and transformation helped shape the future of Canada and solidified his place in the annals of Canadian history.Mulroney's legacy as Prime Minister is multifaceted, encompassing both achievements and challenges. On the one hand, his government implemented bold economic reforms that laid the groundwork for Canada's emergence as a global economic powerhouse. Initiatives such as the negotiation of NAFTA and the privatization of state-owned enterprises helped stimulate investment, create jobs, and expand Canada's export markets. Mulroney's economic policies, though controversial at times, contributed to a period of sustained economic growth and prosperity in Canada.On the other hand, Mulroney's tenure was marked by controversies and challenges, including ethical concerns, environmental issues, and constitutional crises. Scandals such as the Airbus Affair tarnished his reputation and raised questions about integrity and ethics in Canadian politics. Mulroney's handling of environmental issues, particularly the proliferation of acid rain and pollution, drew criticism from environmentalists and advocacy groups. Additionally, his attempts to address constitutional issues, such as Quebec's status within Canada, led to protracted and divisive debates that highlighted deep-seated divisions within the country.Despite these challenges, Mulroney's legacy as Prime Minister is one of significant impact and lasting influence. His government's policies, though divisive, sparked important debates and discussions that continue to shape the country's political landscape. Mulroney's leadership during a period of profound change and transformation helped solidify Canada's position on the global stage and set the stage for future debates and reforms.Continued Engagement: In the years since leaving office, Brian Mulroney has continued to be a prominent figure in Canadian public life, engaging in various activities and initiatives aimed at promoting positive change. He has remained active in charitable work and philanthropy, supporting organizations and causes that align with his values and beliefs. Mulroney has also lent his expertise and experience to various advisory roles and consultancy projects, providing insights and guidance on matters of public policy and governance.Mulroney's continued engagement in public life underscores his ongoing commitment to making a difference in Canadian society. Despite the passage of time and the challenges he has faced, Mulroney remains dedicated to advancing causes he believes in and contributing to the betterment of Canada and the world.Reflections on Leadership: As Brian Mulroney reflects on his life and legacy, he is reminded of the complexities of leadership and the enduring importance of integrity, vision, and dedication to public service. His journey from humble beginnings to the highest office in the land serves as an inspiration to future generations of leaders, reminding them that anyone, regardless of background or circumstance, can make a meaningful difference in the world.Mulroney's experiences in politics have taught him valuable lessons about the challenges and responsibilities of leadership. He understands the importance of ethical governance, transparency, and accountability in public office, and he recognizes the need for leaders to listen to diverse perspectives and work collaboratively to address complex issues.In reflecting on his time in office, Mulroney acknowledges both the successes and shortcomings of his government. While proud of the achievements made during his tenure, he also recognizes the challenges and controversies that marked his time in office. Mulroney remains committed to learning from past mistakes and building on past successes, recognizing that the work of governance is an ongoing process that requires dedication, humility, and a willingness to adapt to changing circumstances.Ultimately, Brian Mulroney's life story is a testament to the power of perseverance, passion, and principled leadership. His legacy will continue to shape the course of Canadian history for generations to come, serving as a beacon of hope and inspiration for all who strive to build a better future for themselves and their communities.

Chapter Seven

Reflections on Leadership and Impact

In this chapter, we delve into the complexities of leadership as exemplified by Brian Mulroney, exploring the enduring impact of his leadership style and the lessons it offers for future generations.The Nature of Leadership: Brian Mulroney's leadership journey is a testament to the multifaceted nature of leadership. From his early days in Baie-Comeau to his tenure as Prime Minister, Mulroney demonstrated a remarkable ability to navigate challenges, inspire others, and effect meaningful change. His leadership style was characterized by a unique blend of vision, determination, and empathy, enabling him to connect with people from all walks of life and mobilize them towards common goals.The Importance of Integrity: Throughout his career, Brian Mulroney placed a high value on integrity and ethical conduct in leadership. He believed that leaders must uphold the highest standards of honesty, transparency, and accountability in their actions, regardless of the challenges they face. Mulroney's unwavering commitment to integrity earned him the trust and respect of the Canadian people, setting an example for future leaders to follow.Navigating Complexity: As Prime Minister, Brian Mulroney faced a myriad of complex issues and competing interests, requiring him to make tough decisions in the best interest of the nation. His ability to navigate these complexities with grace and pragmatism underscores the importance of sound judgment, strategic thinking, and effective decision-making in leadership. Mulroney's approach to governance serves as a valuable case study for leaders grappling with similar challenges in today's rapidly changing world.Empowering Others: One of Brian Mulroney's greatest strengths as a leader was his ability to empower and inspire those around him. He understood that leadership is not about exerting control or authority but rather about fostering collaboration, creativity, and innovation among team members. Mulroney's inclusive leadership style encouraged participation and input from all stakeholders, enabling diverse perspectives to be heard and valued in the decision-making process.Legacy of Leadership: As we reflect on Brian Mulroney's legacy, we are reminded of the enduring impact of his leadership on Canadian politics and society. His vision, integrity, and commitment to public service continue to inspire leaders around the world to strive for excellence and make a positive difference in their communities. Mulroney's legacy serves as a reminder of the transformative power of leadership and the profound impact that one individual can have on the course of history.

Chapter 8

Legacy of Bipartisanship

The Continuing Influence of Brian MulroneyBeyond his time in office, Brian Mulroney's influence continues to resonate in Canadian politics, society, and beyond. As we examine the ongoing impact of his legacy, it becomes evident that Mulroney's contributions extend far beyond his years as Prime Minister.Political Landscape: Brian Mulroney's leadership fundamentally reshaped the political landscape of Canada. His tenure as Prime Minister marked a pivotal moment in Canadian history, during which significant policy changes were implemented, setting the stage for future governments. Mulroney's economic policies, including free trade agreements and privatization initiatives, continue to shape Canada's approach to economic governance. Additionally, his efforts to address constitutional issues, such as Quebec's status within Canada, sparked important debates about national unity and identity that continue to resonate today.Conservative Movement: Mulroney's leadership also had a profound impact on the Conservative movement in Canada. His tenure as leader of the Progressive Conservative Party saw the party achieve unprecedented electoral success, winning back-to-back majority governments in 1984 and 1988. While the party experienced internal divisions and challenges during Mulroney's time in office, his leadership laid the groundwork for future Conservative leaders to build upon. Mulroney's legacy continues to influence the direction and identity of the Conservative Party of Canada, shaping its policies and priorities in the years following his departure from politics.Global Diplomacy: Brian Mulroney's influence extends beyond Canada's borders, with his contributions to international diplomacy and global affairs leaving a lasting impact on the world stage. His close relationship with U.S. Presidents Ronald Reagan and George H.W. Bush strengthened Canada's ties with its southern neighbor and helped advance shared interests on issues such as trade, security, and defense. Mulroney's advocacy for international peacekeeping and cooperation also elevated Canada's role as a key player in global affairs, contributing to efforts to resolve conflicts and promote stability around the world.Philanthropy and Advocacy: In his post-political career, Brian Mulroney has remained active in philanthropy and advocacy, using his platform to support causes he believes in and make a positive impact on Canadian society. He has lent his support to various charitable organizations and initiatives aimed at promoting environmental conservation, social justice, and international peacekeeping. Mulroney's continued engagement in public life underscores his ongoing commitment to making a difference in the world, inspiring others to do the same.Public Perception: Despite facing controversies and challenges during his time in office, Brian Mulroney's public perception has evolved over time.

While he remains a divisive figure in Canadian politics, his contributions to the nation's history are increasingly recognized and acknowledged by Canadians from across the political spectrum. Mulroney's leadership during a period of significant change and transformation continues to be studied and analyzed by scholars, providing valuable insights into the complexities of governance and the challenges of leadership in a democratic society.

Of Economic Policies: Brian Mulroney's economic policies continue to influence Canada's approach to economic governance and international trade. The negotiation and implementation of the North American Free Trade Agreement (NAFTA) transformed Canada's economic landscape, promoting trade liberalization and integration with the United States and Mexico. While NAFTA has faced criticism and renegotiation in subsequent years, its foundational principles of free trade and economic cooperation endure, shaping Canada's position in the global economy.Continued Debate on Constitutional Issues: Mulroney's efforts to address constitutional issues, such as Quebec's status within Canada, sparked enduring debates about national unity and identity. The failure of the Meech Lake and Charlottetown Accords highlighted deep-seated divisions within the country and raised fundamental questions about Canada's federal structure. Despite the challenges of achieving consensus on constitutional reform, Mulroney's legacy underscores the importance of dialogue and negotiation in resolving complex issues of national significance.Environmental Conservation: Mulroney's advocacy for environmental conservation continues to resonate with Canadians concerned about the impacts of climate change and ecological degradation. His leadership on environmental issues helped raise awareness about the importance of protecting Canada's natural heritage and promoting sustainable development. Mulroney's efforts to address environmental challenges serve as a model for future leaders grappling with the urgent need to mitigate climate change and protect biodiversity.Influence on Future Leaders: Brian Mulroney's leadership journey serves as a source of inspiration and guidance for future generations of leaders in Canada and beyond. His ability to navigate complex political challenges with integrity and vision provides valuable lessons for aspiring leaders seeking to make a positive impact on their communities and the world. Mulroney's commitment to public service and advocacy for causes he believes in serves as a model for ethical leadership and principled decision-making.Historical Reflection: As historians continue to assess Mulroney's legacy, his contributions to Canadian politics and society are subject to ongoing analysis and interpretation. Scholars explore the complexities of his leadership, examining both the successes and failures of his government's policies. Through historical reflection, Mulroney's legacy is contextualized within the broader narrative of Canadian history, shedding light on the political, social, and economic dynamics that have shaped the nation's trajectory.Personal Reflection: In his own reflections on his legacy, Brian Mulroney acknowledges the challenges and controversies that marked his time in office, but also takes pride in the accomplishments and contributions of his government. He recognizes the enduring impact of his leadership on Canada's evolution as a nation and remains committed to promoting causes he is passionate about, including environmental conservation and international peacekeeping. Mulroney's personal reflections offer insights into the complexities of leadership and the enduring importance of public service.

Chapter Nine

Commitment to Public Service

The Enduring Influence of Brian MulroneyIn this chapter, we explore the lasting impact of Brian Mulroney's leadership on Canadian politics, society, and beyond. From his visionary policies to his personal integrity, Mulroney's influence continues to shape the course of Canadian history and inspire leaders around the world.Economic Transformation: Brian Mulroney's economic policies laid the groundwork for Canada's emergence as a global economic powerhouse. His bold reforms, including the negotiation of the

North American Free Trade Agreement (NAFTA) and the privatization of state-owned enterprises, helped stimulate investment, create jobs, and expand Canada's export markets. Today, Canada stands as a key player in the global economy, thanks in part to Mulroney's vision and leadership in pursuing free trade and economic liberalization.Environmental Conservation: Mulroney's commitment to environmental conservation and sustainability continues to resonate with Canadians concerned about the impacts of climate change and ecological degradation. His efforts to protect Canada's natural heritage and promote sustainable development set a precedent for future leaders grappling with environmental challenges. Mulroney's advocacy for environmental conservation serves as a model for responsible stewardship of the planet and inspires ongoing efforts to preserve biodiversity and combat climate change.National Unity: Throughout his tenure as Prime Minister, Mulroney worked tirelessly to address the issue of Quebec's status within Canada and promote national unity. While his efforts to secure constitutional reform ultimately proved unsuccessful, Mulroney's commitment to dialogue and compromise helped bridge divides and foster a sense of unity among Canadians. Today, his legacy reminds us of the importance of inclusivity and understanding in building a strong and united nation.Global Leadership: Brian Mulroney's leadership on the global stage elevated Canada's reputation as a respected international actor. His close relationships with world leaders and advocacy for multilateralism helped advance Canada's interests and values on the world stage. Today, Canada continues to play a leading role in international affairs, building on Mulroney's legacy of diplomatic engagement and cooperation.Ethical Governance: Despite facing allegations of ethical impropriety, Mulroney remained steadfast in upholding the highest standards of integrity and ethics in public office. His unwavering commitment to transparency and accountability serves as a model for ethical governance in the public sector. Today, leaders across all levels of government can draw inspiration from Mulroney's example, recognizing the importance of honesty and integrity in serving the public interest.Personal Legacy: Beyond his political accomplishments, Brian Mulroney's personal legacy is one of resilience, determination, and dedication to public service. His journey from humble beginnings to the highest office in the land serves as an inspiration to aspiring leaders, reminding them that anything is possible with hard work and perseverance. Today, Mulroney's legacy continues to inspire individuals from all walks of life to strive for excellence and make a positive difference in their communities.

Legacy of Bipartisanship: Brian Mulroney's ability to work across party lines and build consensus serves as a model for today's leaders grappling with political polarization

and divisiveness. Despite being a leader of
the Progressive Conservative Party,

Chapter Ten

Brian Mulroney's Enduring Legacy

In this concluding chapter, we reflect on the profound impact of Brian Mulroney's leadership and the enduring legacy he leaves behind. From his visionary policies to his personal integrity, Mulroney's contributions have left an indelible mark on Canadian politics and society.A Legacy of Transformation: Brian Mulroney's leadership ushered in an era of transformation and progress in Canada. His bold economic reforms, commitment to environmental conservation, and efforts to promote national unity have shaped the nation's trajectory and set the stage for continued growth and prosperity. Mulroney's legacy serves as a testament to the power of leadership in driving positive change and shaping the future of a nation.Inspiration for Future Leaders: Mulroney's journey from humble beginnings to the highest office in the land serves as an inspiration to aspiring leaders. His resilience, determination, and dedication to public service demonstrate the transformative power of leadership and the potential for individuals to effect meaningful change. Mulroney's legacy inspires future generations of leaders to strive for excellence and make a positive difference in their communities and the world.Lessons for Leadership: Throughout his career, Brian Mulroney exemplified the qualities of effective leadership, including vision, integrity, and perseverance. His ability to navigate complex challenges with grace and dignity serves as a model for leaders across all sectors. Mulroney's legacy offers valuable lessons for leadership, reminding us of the importance of ethical governance, collaboration, and a commitment to serving the greater good.Continued Engagement: Even in retirement, Brian Mulroney remains actively engaged in public life, offering insights and guidance on matters of governance and policy. His ongoing advocacy for causes he believes in, including environmental conservation and international peacekeeping, underscores his enduring commitment to making a positive impact on Canadian society. Mulroney's continued engagement serves as a reminder of the responsibilities that come with leadership and the importance of using one's platform for the betterment of others.A Call to Action: As we reflect on Brian Mulroney's legacy, we are called to action to uphold the values of integrity, inclusivity, and compassion that he embodied throughout his career. Mulroney's legacy challenges us to strive for excellence in our own leadership endeavors and to work tirelessly to build a better, more equitable society for all. His example reminds us that each individual has the power to effect change, and that true leadership is measured not by personal accolades, but by the positive impact we have on the lives of others.Mulroney recognized the importance of reaching out to opposition parties and seeking common ground on key issues. His willingness to collaborate with political rivals demonstrates the power of bipartisanship in achieving meaningful progress and addressing the needs of all Canadians. Today's leaders can learn from Mulroney's example, striving to bridge divides and foster constructive dialogue in pursuit of shared goals.Commitment to Public Service: Throughout his career, Brian Mulroney demonstrated a deep commitment to public service and the well-being of Canadians. His passion for making a positive difference in the lives of others fueled his dedication to leadership and governance. Today's leaders can draw inspiration from Mulroney's commitment to serving the public good, recognizing the profound impact they can have on society through their leadership and actions. By prioritizing the interests of their constituents and serving with humility and compassion, leaders can leave a lasting legacy of positive change and impact.Legacy of Resilience: Brian Mulroney's resilience in the face of adversity serves as a source of inspiration for leaders navigating challenges and setbacks. Despite facing criticism and setbacks during his time in office, Mulroney remained steadfast in pursuing his vision for Canada and addressing the nation's most pressing issues. His ability to persevere in the face of adversity underscores the importance of resilience and determination in leadership. Today's leaders can draw strength from Mulroney's example, recognizing that resilience is essential for overcoming obstacles and achieving long-term success.Continuing Engagement:

Even in retirement, Brian Mulroney remains actively engaged in public life, offering insights and guidance on matters of governance and policy. His continued involvement in philanthropy, advocacy, and public discourse underscores his ongoing commitment to making a positive impact on Canadian society. Today's leaders can benefit from Mulroney's wisdom and experience, seeking out opportunities to learn from his insights and engage in meaningful dialogue on issues of mutual interest. By leveraging the expertise of former leaders like Mulroney, current leaders can gain valuable perspectives and insights that inform their decision-making and shape their approach to leadership.Inspiring Future Generations: Brian Mulroney's legacy serves as an inspiration for future generations of leaders, motivating them to strive for excellence and make a positive difference in the world. His journey from humble beginnings to the highest office in the land demonstrates the transformative power of leadership and the potential for individuals to effect meaningful change. Today's leaders can draw inspiration from Mulroney's example, embracing the challenges and opportunities of leadership with courage, integrity, and a commitment to serving the greater good.

Honoring a Legacy: As we conclude our exploration of Brian Mulroney's legacy, it is essential to acknowledge the significance of honoring his contributions to Canadian society. Through monuments, museums, scholarships, and other forms of recognition, Canadians can ensure that Mulroney's impact is remembered and celebrated for generations to come. By commemorating his achievements, we not only pay tribute to a remarkable leader but also inspire future generations to follow in his footsteps and continue his legacy of excellence and service.Continuing the Conversation: The legacy of Brian Mulroney is not static; it is a dynamic and evolving narrative that continues to shape the discourse on leadership, governance, and public service in Canada and beyond. As we move forward, it is imperative to continue the conversation about Mulroney's contributions, examining their significance in the context of contemporary challenges and opportunities. By critically evaluating Mulroney's legacy and drawing lessons from his leadership journey, we can inform our approach to addressing present-day issues and building a brighter future for all Canadians.Looking Ahead: While Brian Mulroney's time in office has come to an end, his influence and impact endure. As Canada faces new challenges and opportunities in the 21st century, we can draw inspiration from Mulroney's example and apply the lessons learned from his leadership to chart a course forward. By embracing the values of integrity, inclusivity, and innovation that Mulroney embodied, we can navigate the complexities of a rapidly changing world with confidence and determination.Gratitude and Appreciation: Finally, it is essential to express gratitude and appreciation for Brian Mulroney's decades of service to Canada. As a leader, statesman, and advocate, Mulroney dedicated himself to advancing the interests of his country and its people with passion, dedication, and integrity. While his legacy may be subject to debate and interpretation, there is no denying the profound impact he has had on the course of Canadian history and the lives of countless individuals. As we bid farewell to Brian Mulroney, we do so with gratitude for his leadership, admiration for his accomplishments, and hope for the future he helped shape. Enduring lessons from Brian Mulroney's leadership is the importance of embracing diversity and inclusion. Throughout his career, Mulroney championed policies and initiatives aimed at promoting equality and respecting the rights of all Canadians, regardless of their background or identity. His commitment to multiculturalism and inclusivity helped shape Canada into a more tolerant and diverse society. As we continue to navigate the complexities of a multicultural world, Mulroney's example serves as a guiding light, reminding us of the importance of embracing diversity and fostering a culture of inclusion in all aspects of society.Fostering Civic Engagement: Brian Mulroney's leadership style was characterized by a deep respect for democratic values and principles. He understood the importance of active citizenship and civic engagement in a vibrant democracy, and he encouraged Canadians to participate in the political process and contribute to the betterment of their communities. Mulroney's legacy reminds us that democracy is not a passive endeavor but rather a collective responsibility that requires active participation and engagement from all members of society. By fostering a culture of civic engagement and participation, we can uphold the democratic ideals that Mulroney held dear and ensure that our political system remains responsive and accountable to the needs of all Canadians.Continuing the Conversation: As we reflect on Brian Mulroney's legacy, it is essential to recognize that his impact extends far beyond his time in office. Mulroney's leadership journey is a rich tapestry of triumphs and challenges, successes and setbacks, all of which offer valuable insights and lessons for leaders in the present day and beyond. By continuing the conversation about Mulroney's legacy and engaging in meaningful dialogue about the issues and values that he stood for, we can ensure that his contributions are not forgotten and that his vision for Canada continues to inspire and guide us in the years to come.A Call to Action: Ultimately, Brian Mulroney's legacy is not just a reflection of the past but also a call to action for the future. His example challenges us to aspire to greatness, to strive for excellence, and to make a positive difference in the world around us. Whether through public service, advocacy, or community activism, each of us has the power to contribute to the betterment of society in our own unique way. As we honor Mulroney's legacy and reflect on his contributions, let us also recommit ourselves to the values of leadership, integrity, and service that he embodied, ensuring that his impact continues to be felt for generations to come.

Chapter Eleven

Mulroney's Role in NAFTA Negotiations

In the midst of ongoing NAFTA negotiations and geopolitical uncertainty, the guidance provided by former Prime Minister Brian Mulroney holds significant relevance. Mulroney's adept negotiation skills and strategic approach to diplomacy continue to shape Canada's international relations, particularly in trade agreements like NAFTA. This chapter explores the enduring legacy of Mulroney's leadership and the lessons it offers for contemporary policymakers.

Brian Mulroney's tenure as Prime Minister marked a pivotal period in Canada's trade relations, culminating in the negotiation of NAFTA. As the architect of NAFTA's predecessor, the Canada-U.S. Free Trade Agreement, Mulroney laid the groundwork for deeper economic integration with our southern neighbor. His steadfast commitment to securing beneficial trade deals for Canada serves as a guiding principle for current negotiators, emphasizing the importance of prioritizing national interests in trade agreements. Mulroney's leadership during NAFTA negotiations was characterized by a strategic approach that balanced assertiveness with pragmatism. Recognizing the significance of the North American market for Canada's economic prosperity, Mulroney advocated for a comprehensive trade agreement that would eliminate barriers to trade and investment across borders. His vision for NAFTA was grounded in the belief that increased economic cooperation would benefit all parties involved, leading to greater prosperity and shared opportunities for growth.Despite facing resistance from domestic opponents and navigating complex negotiations with the United States and Mexico, Mulroney remained resolute in his pursuit of a mutually beneficial trade agreement. His determination to secure a deal that protected Canadian interests while fostering closer ties with our North American partners was evident throughout the negotiation process.Mulroney's approach to NAFTA negotiations was guided by the principle that "no deal is better than a bad deal." This mantra underscored his commitment to securing favorable terms for Canada, even if it meant walking away from the negotiating table. By prioritizing the long-term interests of the Canadian economy over short-term concessions, Mulroney demonstrated leadership and resolve in advancing Canada's position in international trade negotiations.Today, as Canada grapples with the renegotiation of NAFTA and the evolving dynamics of global trade, the lessons learned from Mulroney's leadership remain as relevant as ever. His strategic vision, principled approach, and unwavering commitment to Canadian interests serve as a blueprint for navigating complex trade negotiations in an increasingly interconnected world. As policymakers seek to uphold Canada's economic prosperity and competitiveness on the global stage, Mulroney's legacy continues to provide invaluable insights and guidance for charting a course towards a more prosperous and sustainable future.

In addition to his strategic vision and principled approach, Brian Mulroney's leadership during NAFTA negotiations was characterized by his ability to forge strong relationships with key stakeholders, both domestically and internationally. Recognizing the importance of consensus-building and collaboration, Mulroney engaged in extensive consultations with provincial governments, industry representatives, and other stakeholders to ensure broad-based support for the trade agreement.Mulroney's leadership style was marked by inclusivity and transparency, as he sought to engage Canadians in the process of negotiating NAFTA and address their concerns. By fostering open dialogue and soliciting feedback from diverse perspectives, Mulroney demonstrated a commitment to democratic governance and accountability. Furthermore, Mulroney's diplomatic skills and political acumen were instrumental in overcoming obstacles and reaching compromises during NAFTA negotiations. His ability to navigate complex political dynamics and bridge ideological divides enabled him to build consensus and advance Canada's interests on the international stage. Moreover, Mulroney's leadership during NAFTA negotiations showcased

Canada's capacity to play a proactive and constructive role in shaping the global trade agenda. By championing the principles of free trade and economic integration, Mulroney positioned Canada as a key player in the international trade arena, contributing to the advancement of a rules-based global trading system.As Canada continues to navigate the complexities of global trade and renegotiate NAFTA in the 21st century, the lessons learned from Mulroney's leadership remain invaluable. His strategic vision, inclusive approach, and commitment to advancing Canadian interests serve as a blueprint for effective leadership in international negotiations. By drawing upon Mulroney's legacy, Canadian policymakers can navigate the challenges and opportunities of the modern global economy with confidence and resilience, ensuring continued prosperity and success for future generations. Brian Mulroney's leadership during NAFTA negotiations highlighted the importance of building strong alliances and leveraging Canada's position as a middle power to advance its interests on the world stage. Mulroney recognized the strategic value of aligning with like-minded partners and building coalitions to amplify Canada's voice and influence in international trade discussions.During NAFTA negotiations, Mulroney worked closely with other Western Hemisphere leaders, including Presidents George H.W. Bush of the United States and Carlos Salinas de Gortari of Mexico, to build consensus and overcome contentious issues. By fostering a spirit of cooperation and collaboration among NAFTA member countries, Mulroney facilitated the successful conclusion of the trade agreement and laid the groundwork for a new era of economic integration in North America.

Brian Mulroney's leadership during NAFTA negotiations serves as a testament to the power of strategic vision, collaborative diplomacy, and proactive engagement in shaping the course of international trade. Mulroney's legacy as a master negotiator and advocate for free trade continues to resonate today, providing valuable lessons for policymakers seeking to navigate the complexities of the global economy and secure Canada's prosperity in an increasingly interconnected world. As

Canada embarks on a new chapter in its trade relations, Mulroney's example serves as a source of inspiration and guidance for charting a path towards a more prosperous and sustainable future for all Canadians.

Chapter Twelve

Mulroney's "Activist" International Policy

Brian Mulroney's leadership extended beyond economic matters to encompass a broader vision of Canada's role in global affairs. As Prime Minister, Mulroney pursued an "activist" foreign policy agenda that prioritized Canada's engagement in international humanitarian efforts, advocacy for human rights, and promotion of global peace and stability.One of Mulroney's notable contributions to international affairs was Canada's response to the famine crisis in Ethiopia during the mid-1980s. Recognizing the severity of the humanitarian crisis, Mulroney mobilized Canadian resources and worked with the international community to provide humanitarian aid to alleviate suffering and save lives. Canada's leadership in responding to the Ethiopian famine underscored Mulroney's commitment to addressing global challenges and promoting humanitarian values on the world stage.

Brian Mulroney's efforts and ambition in advancing Canada's "activist" international policy were evident in his proactive approach to addressing global challenges and championing humanitarian causes on the world stage. As Prime Minister, Mulroney demonstrated a strong commitment to promoting Canada's values of peace, human rights, and environmental sustainability, leveraging Canada's influence to effect meaningful change and make a positive impact on pressing global issues.One of Mulroney's ambitious endeavors was his leadership in advocating for sanctions against apartheid South Africa. Recognizing the moral imperative to oppose apartheid and support the struggle for equality and justice in South Africa, Mulroney took a principled stand against the oppressive regime and mobilized international support for sanctions. Despite facing resistance from some international partners, Mulroney remained steadfast in his commitment to ending apartheid and advancing the cause of freedom and equality for all South Africans.Moreover, Mulroney's ambition in addressing global environmental challenges was evident in his advocacy for the reduction of acid rain emissions through international cooperation. Recognizing the harmful impact of acid rain on ecosystems and human health, Mulroney took proactive steps to address this pressing environmental issue, leading to the negotiation of the Acid Rain Treaty with the United States. By championing international cooperation and diplomacy on environmental protection, Mulroney demonstrated his ambition to safeguard the planet for future generations and promote sustainable development.Mulroney's ambition extended to his efforts in providing humanitarian assistance to countries in crisis, such as Ethiopia during the famine of the mid-1980s. Recognizing the urgent need for international support to alleviate suffering and save lives, Mulroney mobilized Canadian resources and worked with the international community to provide humanitarian aid to Ethiopia. His ambitious efforts to address the humanitarian crisis reflected Canada's commitment to global solidarity and compassion in the face of adversity. Mulroney's ambition extended to his efforts in providing humanitarian assistance to countries in crisis, such as Ethiopia during the famine of the mid-1980s. Recognizing the urgent need for international support to alleviate suffering and save lives, Mulroney mobilized Canadian resources and worked with the international community to provide humanitarian aid to Ethiopia, demonstrating Canada's commitment to global solidarity and humanitarian action in times of crisis.

Overall, Brian Mulroney's ambition in advancing Canada's "activist" international policy underscored his commitment to making a meaningful impact on the world stage and promoting Canada's values and interests abroad. Through his bold leadership and decisive action, Mulroney left a lasting legacy of Canadian leadership in global affairs, demonstrating the importance of ambition, determination, and principled leadership in addressing complex global challenges and advancing the cause of peace, justice, and sustainability.

Chapter Thirteen

Legacy and Enduring Influence

We delve into the enduring impact of Brian Mulroney's leadership on Canada and the world. As we reflect on his tenure as Prime Minister, we are reminded of the remarkable achievements, challenges overcome, and the lasting legacy he has left behind.

Economic Legacy: Brian Mulroney's economic policies transformed Canada's economy, ushering in an era of globalization and trade liberalization. His pivotal role in negotiating the North American Free Trade Agreement (NAFTA) and the Canada-U.S.

Free Trade Agreement (CUSFTA) opened new avenues for economic growth and prosperity, positioning Canada as a key player in the global marketplace. Mulroney's commitment to fiscal responsibility and structural reform laid the foundation for decades of economic stability and growth in Canada. In addition to NAFTA, Mulroney pursued a broader agenda of trade liberalization, seeking to reduce barriers to international trade and investment. His government negotiated numerous bilateral and multilateral trade agreements, opening new markets for Canadian exporters and attracting foreign investment to Canada. Mulroney's commitment to free trade positioned Canada as a global leader in economic openness and competitiveness.

Social Impact: Mulroney's leadership had a profound impact on Canadian society, shaping debates on issues ranging from Indigenous rights to environmental conservation. His government's efforts to address social inequalities and promote inclusivity left a lasting imprint on Canadian society, fostering a more equitable and compassionate nation. Mulroney's commitment to multiculturalism and diversity reflected Canada's values as a welcoming and inclusive society.3. Political Legacy: As Prime Minister, Brian Mulroney faced numerous challenges and controversies, but his legacy as a transformative leader endures. His ability to navigate complex political terrain and build consensus across party lines demonstrated his statesmanship and leadership skills.

Mulroney's contributions to constitutional reform, Indigenous reconciliation, and national unity continue to shape Canadian politics and governance.4. International Influence: Mulroney's influence extended beyond Canada's borders, as he played a prominent role in global affairs. His advocacy for human rights, environmental protection, and peacekeeping efforts earned Canada respect and admiration on the world stage. Mulroney's diplomatic acumen and strategic vision elevated Canada's international standing, reaffirming its role as a trusted partner and mediator in global conflicts.

Chapter fourteen

Reflections and Continuity

In this final chapter, we reflect on Brian Mulroney's legacy and its enduring significance for Canada and the world. As we conclude our exploration of his life and leadership, we consider the lessons learned, the challenges faced, and the ongoing relevance of Mulroney's vision for the future.

Legacy of Leadership: Brian Mulroney's legacy as a leader is characterized by his vision, determination, and commitment to public service. Throughout his career, he demonstrated an unwavering dedication to advancing the interests of Canadians and promoting Canada's role on the world stage.

His leadership style, characterized by pragmatism, diplomacy, and strategic thinking, continues to inspire current and future leaders.

Lessons Learned: The Mulroney era offers valuable lessons for policymakers and leaders alike. His ability to navigate complex political terrain, build consensus across party lines, and pursue bold initiatives in the face of opposition underscores the importance of leadership in times of change and uncertainty. Mulroney's emphasis on dialogue, compromise, and principled decision-making serves as a model for effective governance in a diverse and dynamic society.

Challenges Overcome: Mulroney faced numerous challenges and controversies during his tenure as Prime Minister, from economic recessions to constitutional crises. However, his resilience, tenacity, and ability to rise above adversity enabled him to overcome these challenges and leave a lasting impact on Canadian politics and society. Mulroney's willingness to confront difficult issues and pursue ambitious goals demonstrates the transformative power of leadership in times of crisis.

Ongoing Relevance: Despite the passage of time, Brian Mulroney's legacy remains relevant in today's political landscape. His contributions to economic prosperity, social justice, and international diplomacy continue to shape Canada's policies and priorities. As Canada confronts new challenges and opportunities in the 21st century, Mulroney's vision for a strong, prosperous, and inclusive nation serves as a guiding light for future generations.

Continuity and Change: As we look to the future, it is essential to build upon the foundation laid by Brian Mulroney and his government. While the world may have changed since his time in office, the fundamental values of integrity, compassion, and service to others remain as relevant as ever. By embracing continuity and change, Canada can continue to honor Mulroney's legacy while adapting to the evolving needs of society.

Conclusion: In conclusion, Brian Mulroney's legacy is one of leadership, resilience, and vision. His contributions to Canada and the world have left an indelible mark on history, inspiring generations of leaders to strive for excellence and pursue the common good. As we reflect on Mulroney's life and leadership, we are reminded of the enduring importance of integrity, courage, and compassion in shaping a better future for all. May his legacy continue to inspire and guide us in the years to come.

Chapter Fifteen

Honoring Brian Mulroney's Legacy

In the wake of Brian Mulroney's passing, the nation mourns the loss of a true statesman and visionary leader. As Canadians come together to pay tribute to his remarkable legacy, we extend our deepest condolences to his family, friends, and loved ones.Brian Mulroney's contributions to Canada and the world are immeasurable, spanning decades of dedicated service and principled leadership. From his transformative economic policies to his steadfast commitment to social justice and human rights, Mulroney leaves behind a legacy of integrity, compassion, and excellence.As we reflect on Mulroney's life and legacy, we are reminded of the profound impact he had on shaping the course of Canadian history. His vision for a more prosperous, inclusive, and compassionate nation inspired countless individuals and continues to resonate with Canadians from coast to coast.In this time of mourning, let us honor Brian Mulroney's memory by embracing the values he held dear: integrity, courage, and a relentless dedication to the common good. May his legacy serve as a guiding light for future generations, inspiring us to strive for excellence and to always put the needs of others before our own.To the Mulroney family, we offer our sincerest condolences and deepest sympathies. May you find comfort in the knowledge that Brian's legacy will live on in the hearts and minds of all Canadians, forever remembered and cherished as a beacon of hope and inspiration. Rest in peace, Brian Mulroney. Your legacy will endure, and your spirit will continue to guide us as we strive to build a better, more compassionate world for all.